I0201932

Essay about the art of embracing people

Argentine tango and Coaching

Adrián Luna

adrianlunacoach.com

Luna, Adrián Héctor
  Essay about the art of embracing people : Argentine tango and coaching
/ Adrián Héctor Luna ; contribuciones de Mora Noel Sánchez ; fotografías
de Ekaterina Duginova. - 1a ed . - Carlos Casares : Adrián Héctor Luna,
2018.
  152 p. ; 22 x 15 cm.

  ISBN 978-987-42-9533-0

  1. Tango. 2. Coaching. 3. Marketing Turístico. I. Sánchez, Mora Noel,
colab. II. Duginova, Ekaterina, fot. III. Título.
  CDD 793.31

1st Edition: September 2018

Author: Adrián Luna
ISBN: 978-987-42-9533-0
Dancer and Model: Mora Noel Sánchez
Photographer: Ekaterina Duginova
Cover design: Adrián Luna
Interior design: Adrián Luna

No part of this publication may be reproduced, stored in or introduced into a
retrieval system, or transmitted, in any form, or by any means (electronic,
mechanical, photocopying, recording, or otherwise), without the prior
permission of the author.

Index

Acknowledgments

I want to thank my parents, Mirta and Armando, my grandmother Ives, and my friends for all their support in making this book come true. Special recognition goes to my friends, Nelba Castagnasso and Carlos Grijalba Zabala, for the nights of analysis and debate on most of the topics discussed here. To my friend Pablo Clariá for his technical contributions and his dedicated feedback throughout the process of creating this work. To Valeria Pina and her lovely family always ready and willing to help me. To Regina Satz for sharing her experience and vision of tango. And especially to Mora Noel Sánchez for being a source of inspiration, her trust, her infinite love, for believing and then creating.

A few words of wisdom

This is not a tango book, nor about how to learn the steps to dance tango in Buenos Aires. This is a book about people, human beings who embrace and relate in a very particular way in an "environment" with their own rules.

In the coach, I find a professional and appropriate figure to accompany us in learning this "language." I consider it appropriate to compare him with a gardener who knows about the weather, the seasons and irrigation techniques, among many other things. It is taken with seriousness and professionalism to prepare the ground to offer the seed the conditions that satisfy and accompany its development. He is a great observer and takes into account even the smallest details. However, he has confidence and believes in the potential that exists within the seed. He doesn't need to see what it has inside or check how much fruit it's going to produce... This mystery seems wonderful to me and is revealed little by little during the process of germination and growth.

This essay is, on the one hand, for those who are "gardeners" by vocation, with whom I wish to seriously develop this activity. On the other hand, it's for those people who want to learn to dance the tango and have no idea where or who to start with.

Through this path we can end up getting to know ourselves a little more. Be attentive!

Foreword

The tango found me back in 1996. I danced choreographies on my city's stages, as well as those of several provinces, such as La Pampa, Santiago del Estero and San Luis. When I came to live in Buenos Aires, I went dancing at a milonga and discovered that I didn't know anything about what I thought I knew. I had been doing something different for about two years, along with the group I knew how to integrate with.

> *I had been dancing choreographies.*

With deep pain (to my pride) I began to take beginner level lessons, to learn what I already thought I knew. I took a number of group classes and wandered through different places to do it. It was a pilgrimage that always ended in a feeling of emptiness. I began to feel that this void was beyond my physical prowess with respect to the figures and that was when I decided to hire a special "teacher" to guide me. Then the disillusion was even greater; suffice it to say that I paid for 20 classes and decided not to take the last one.

> *Nobody, throughout my entire experience, suggested that I listen to tangos.*

11

My parents belong to the rock generation, so when I was a kid at home you couldn't hear tango. Fortunately, during my search I discovered that listening to tangos offered an extraordinary advantage for better dancing. Little by little I became interested in the different orchestras and slowly began to nest emotions in my solar plexus. These emotions found a channel to flow through when I embraced to dance. I quickly understood the value of emotions when relating to another person in a "tango hug."

I think it was when I started *loving* the tango that I started dancing. All the above was necessary, but I cannot consider nor approximate what it means for me to listen and dance the tango socially, improvising in a milonga.

I have cried a lot and suffered my learning like few things in life. However, after having paid the price, tango has given me many of the greatest experiences and opportunities of my life.

As soon as I started to enjoy it, I began to meet people with similar experiences.

Unfortunately, many of them finally left the tango.

The objective of this work is to question and challenge the current model, and to analyze the world and the cultural industry, by adding some variables that, I think, are not on the radar of those who "do the tango."

You will find a list of ideas, here, thoughts, heartaches and observations that I have been experiencing as a learner, social dancer and coach. You will also find, at the end of the work, a brief glossary that defines the most commonly used terms in the world of tango.

It took a long time to complete this work because it took me recognizing that I wanted to have some "certainty" to be able to write something serious, valid or that it simply was worthwhile.

Far from it, I've managed to write it with the conviction of wanting to correct it shortly after I printed it. The amendments will probably not only be mine but of those who have looked at it who will help to cement certain aspects that, in my opinion, are taken for granted. I hope that it will open up the debate.

Observations

Touring and observing the different milongas, practices and schools of tango - some of which I call "step schools" - you can find conditions that, in my opinion, are an obstacle to the promotion of tango and the effective communication of its benefits:

- Some tango "teachers" know almost nothing of the music they dance to or its history, and some don't even attend the milongas.

- The "teachers" do not advise their students that there are different styles - Salon, Canyengue, Milonguero, Modern, etc., so that every student who does not identify with the style dictated by the teacher leaves tango as a genre.

- Group classes are usually "step classes" where social, emotional and musical aspects are practically not even taken into account.

- Some of the great tango dancers became the main masters. One who is an expert in an art is not necessarily a good teacher. In tango, this is quite common, where pedagogy and communication skills are lacking or scarce. The technical capacity of the person who is instructing the class is almost the only qualifying factor or, simply, for having lived in "that golden age."

- Professional dancers of other dances, having little work and/or students, discovered a great work opportunity in tango, quoted in dollars and with international projection. They, having developed physical and technical skills, can easily copy the steps of the tango and begin to teach them. The problem is that they don't know, nor do they care, about the essential gender issues that make what they communicate sustainable in time.

- Some professional tango dancers, having no work on stage, are forced to give classes to survive. But they do it out of necessity and not by vocation, because if they could receive remuneration just for dancing, they wouldn't teach such classes. This has an enormous impact on the quality of the lessons they offer, since they don't like the idea of "dealing" with the most basic tango figures with beginner or intermediate students.

Clarification

In the tango community there are great dancers who are also great teachers and have a strong vocation, as well as having a wide knowledge of tango and the culture. I'm just saying that sometimes there's no distinction between one and the other, this being very harmful for the whole community, its growth and promotion.

Tango and coaching

The difference between stage tango and social tango

It's worth taking the time to distinguish between these two concepts, as sometimes the difference isn't clear.

Stage tango is danced by professional dancers who train, have choreography, period costumes, directors, producers and (depending on the budget) everything an artist needs to show to the audience present, which usually has the passive role of observing the show.

Social tango is the one that (in its majority) is danced by people who haven't dedicated themselves professionally to dancing, nor do they want to. They are people who go to "milonguear (dance the milonga)" and don't worry about showing up in public. They want to enjoy the experience of what it means to dance the tango, embrace, follow the rhythm and flow together with other couples.

They are aware of what going to dance tango brings to their lives and they are more focused on *feeling* than on *showing off*.

What qualities should a person have who teaches how to dance social tango?

From my observations, I came to the conclusion that more people are needed who want to share the tango with new audiences and take responsibility for what that means.

The following is a tentative list that I consider incomplete and partial, which I hope can be revised to give the community a better standard that allows tango to grow and develop as a direct function of the service and the value it adds to society:

- Being a social dancer: This is part of the milonguero community, in order to instruct in the milonguero codes, to gain knowledge of the risks and the advantages within the milonguero "game," and to have lived and experienced it personally.

- Dance knowledge: The one who wants to instruct should know how to dance and be able to demonstrate it on the dance floor. Knowing different styles gives you the opportunity to provide a better and more varied offer to your apprentices/students.

- Knowledge of the music: To dance the tango you have to listen to it; otherwise it's just movements with a certain technical capacity within a rhythm (which could well be any other music). The coach has to *feel* the music and know the styles, times and impact that many orchestras generate in the minds of people.

- Being human: Knowledge of the importance of human relationships above the accomplishment of the performance during the practice. Knowing how to take care of others while they learn, is to say that they can "survive" learning.

- Listen to the apprentice: Know their motivations, their needs, the budget for time, energy, money and the expectations they have regarding the tango in their life.

- History: When we're told an anecdote related to a tango, it's impossible not to dance with the imprint and the emotion that this generates. We are part of that story while we dance, and when we listen to it, it activates within us a deeper way of expressing ourselves as we embrace the other.

- Related arts: Tango involves other arts, such as poetry, music, theater, film, painting, sculpture, among many others. Knowing and sharing them greatly enriches the learning experience.

- Love and passion: When you are in love you wear an aura that is contagious. Putting *love and passion* in what you do will guard against all the distances that may arise, no matter what part of the world your partner is in... Love transcends all borders, builds trust and gives us enough power to overcome the obstacles that are presented to us during a journey that lasts a lifetime.

- Calling: Being a coach requires a calling, a genuine desire to accompany the other in a process that is unique to each person. Being able to "love" those who are learning gives us the patience, tolerance and willpower necessary to facilitate learning and discovering their own style. It is a wonderful desire to share and trust in the other's ability to discover tango on its own.

- Knowing how to say "no." Sometimes, by necessity, we may be doing something we do not want or desire, and it's even worse when we do it convinced of a negative result. Choosing who we want to work with dignifies us and gives us the necessary freedom that this type of work requires to achieve valuable, transcendent and lasting results.

- Confidentiality: Be aware of the degree of intimacy that can be achieved. The coaches often see vulnerable people, we notice them outside their comfort zone, insecure, and their glances allow us to deduce that they feel "naked" in front of us. Many emotions emerge from the depths of their being; some are extraordinarily "logical" and show them that tango dancing is not linear learning. To be able to recognize this responsibility I think is the first step in considering whether we are qualified to deal with this type of situation and accompany the apprentice in a responsible and professional way. Coaches often see married couples and in a few practice steps we can perceive a large amount of information about the relationship that exists between them. This is not conclusive, but many times they notice it and feel that they are being observed beyond the tango form in question. That they can *trust* us, that they feel that we are going to respect and take care of what happens within the framework of our meeting, is fundamental for the learning process to take shape.

Example: There are couples who, no matter how many wrong steps they make, give a smile but never leave the embrace. They began with the embrace and do not leave the other for any reason if it is not asked for. Others, before any "wrong" step, separate and look to the coach as a referee to define whose "fault" it is. Having this type of situation in mind and being able to overcome it may be a reason to write a whole book on this particular point.

- Transformation: Recognize that learning tango can be a transformative process, and, as such, respect the times and decisions of the client. For many of us there is a before and after tango.

- Be sensitive to the flow of the day: The coach should be as aware as possible of everything that happens or stops happening from when he meets the client until he leaves. This doesn't mean that he gives you *feedback* on every thing and action perceived: if the client looks at the time every five minutes (this can indicate something we can check in some way), if he yawns, if he looks up or emits irregular gestures. Nothing is determinant in itself, but it's good to pay attention, read and evaluate the behavior of the other, adapt and offer the best possible learning model. It's not our job to tell him *how*, nor *what*, nor *when*, but our function is to question him, asking him questions that lead him to reflection and that allow him to glean the best answers from his own reflections, which are his.

Example: Sometimes I turn around to pour myself some water, to "adjust" something or to check the playlist. Actually, I am giving them a chance to relax the tension that comes from having someone staring at them for so long. They have an opportunity to complain or whisper something (if they're a couple), to smile or simply to be wrong (usually we don't want to be wrong, much less in front of others). This allows them to relax the tension generated.

- Be careful in the use of "labels." When customers are beginners and they are presented with the "names" of each figure, they function as "labels" that they will tend to relate to the actions. Considering that it is a type of dance that is *improvised*, it is a great method to keep the labels as long as possible, or at least until they are the ones who discover them. That saves them the process of trying to label each movement, trying to anticipate it (going forward), instead of living and enjoying the present.

- Communication: The voice, its volume, the speed of speaking, the language, the silences or spaces for reflection. Facial expressions, movements, body language and the different positions that condition communication between the parties are also a determining factor if they are given sufficient attention. There is a large amount of literature on the subject, which always comes in handy for those of us who work with communication between people, much more for coaches, who communicates with the body and through a embrace.

- Hygiene: It is worth clarifying that hygiene is essential, paying attention to basic habits, such as brushing our teeth or washing our hands (especially if we go to the client's house). It's necessary to be aware that dancing can cause a lot of perspiration and that certain types of textures in clothing are less favorable than others to carry out the activity. Be aware that we are going to embrace another person and that the respect we offer them is also the same as what we have for ourselves.

Personal hygiene is a fundamental and determining factor that can never be emphasized enough, after countless unpleasant stories regarding this matter.

- Uniform: Have a wardrobe that identifies us. This is good even for self promotion, for hygiene and to define a style that also includes the way of dressing.

- Sense of humor: Being able to break the ice, desconstruct certain situations, be spontaneous with comments and knowing how to "intervene" opportunely are the most valuable qualities we can have. Using them for the benefit of the participants constitutes great added value for the activity.

Tango as a cultural value vs "Step teachers"

> *Tango is not in the feet; it's in the heart.*

The cultural value of tango is recognized by people from all over the world who dance and enjoy it. However, we still find "step teachers" or "tango step schools" that have little of the milonguera culture and the cultural values that make it up. Without wishing to detract, since there are figures that require a masterful technique - but bearing in mind that the objective of this book is to promote tango by initiating new social dancers - we can agree that not many people are willing to invest time and money in learning skills that they do not identify with (or that come from other dances and are "put" into tango because they sell).

Fortunately, there is room for everyone. I just think it's useful to be able to recognize the role we play in the tango industry by offering something to society. Even if we participate at different levels, be conscientious at every moment to clearly communicate what we are offering and for what audience.

I wonder: "If most of the tango figures can be found on the Internet, why would someone hire a coach?

Gender and roles

Today, fortunately, at least in tango, we are on a level playing field between men and women. It's very good to be aware that the two people who are on the dance floor, regardless of their gender, are in agreement about the role that each of them will play.

I like the image of an invitation to speak of the "signals" by the "leader," that is, the person who assumes the role of leader, who does not carry, push, direct or command whoever assumes the role of follower.

It is well to clarify that when we speak of "signals," we refer to the stimulus emitted by the person who assumes the role of leader to propose a movement to whoever assumes the role of *follower*.

In my opinion, one is the person who chooses to invite the other person to walk together and it is the other person who chooses (in each step) to accept or to decline the invitation.

With regard to language, I think we still need to coin new terms that fit the current reality, overcoming the archaic "leader" and *follower*. Anyway, although it is paradoxical, I will use them because they are accepted in the general vocabulary at the international level. Fortunately, the debate has been open for some time now, so I hope we'll soon have a social consensus.

Roles

Learning tango is normally non-linear, contrary to the logic to which we are accustomed. To tango dance improvising in a milonga, surrounded by other couples (also improvising movements) following the beat, we need skills that are not the result of 1 + 1.

To balance the scales during the dance, both roles will be opposite and complementary, in a proportion that fits each step and at each encounter.

The leader must:

- Have 360 ° perception, be aware of the movements and energy flow of the couples around you. Threats and opportunities (for example, the permanent threat of some of the ladies' stiletto heels).
- Offer your partner a safe space to tread.
- Know where you want to go.
- Be clear in your signals, keeping consistency so that your partner can establish a pattern and understand the suggestions in real time.
- Have very sensitive and effective perception regarding the body feedback your partner sends to you. Recognize this even if you're demanding

space or time to embellish or, perhaps, to get in tempo with the music.

- Recognize the music, orchestra or at least the style that the DJ suggests during the session, in order to adapt your embrace and form of expression.

The role of *follower*:

- Be sensitive to the signals and energy suggested by your partner.
- Don't predict where your partner wants to go.
- Stay in tempo.
- Recognize the spaces and times that are offered to embellish or express yourself as you desire.
- Be able to ask (without words) for the time and space you need (or want).
- Recognize the rhythm of the orchestra or the DJ's suggestions to be able to adapt your embrace and the emotion that this entails.

Clarification:
Throughout the book we will use the terms leader/follower, man/woman and partner because a neutral term has not yet been coined with a general consensus in the tango community. This is independent of the gender of the people who are dancing, where each one exercises a different role.

Tango in schools (human values)

Tango, in its richness, offers us a vast field in which to work, experiment and develop a great diversity of themes. One of them is the hope of using it as a vehicle to work with *universal human values*, to talk about them, to integrate them and to become aware of their importance in society.

We've had a wonderful experience tango dancing with elementary school students, where we share "tango days" with children from 1st to 7th grade, including teachers, principals and auxiliary staff. Due to lack of time, we could not share with parents, but I think that in the future that's an important factor to integrate and implement.

Learn to *make an offer* (to dance in this case), that can be accepted or declined. To choose and be chosen. To thank, generate empathy and recognize the right of the other to choose, to apologize if we collide, to ask permission. Take care of our dance partner when we're leaders, accept that they are guiding us if we're in the role of follower. To build self-confidence and with others, to respect their space and different forms of expression, recognizing the importance of the diversity of expression in a society.

During these sessions we are in a space of equality among teachers, students and assistants. Everyone on the dance floor has the same status.

Tango is an artistic expression that unites us as a society and a cultural space conducive to developing values that can be applied in the rest of the "scenarios" of people's everyday lives.

The Basic Steps

In the teaching of tango there are new emerging models where the forms and structures that were useful in the past no longer are. This is due to the global social and cultural changes that have occurred. Information and communications, today, are on a totally different plane from the past. The means and forms of entertainment have evolved. This leads us to think of an integrated and multimedia model, where the contents come from different sources, in moments and degrees that vary according to the emotional circumstances and the proposed objective starting out.

In addition to leaving aside the structure of the basic tango steps that condition and limit, we are going to focus on the "embrace," which is where the communication between the dancers is centralized, and infinite forms of interpretation of the music can emerge.

Dancing in a milonga, we'll surely have the space that we're occupying in the present time, that is, the diameter of our embrace. That's the only certain thing that we have. It is the function of the leader to manage that space and - when couples are moving on the dance floor - find the place where they can walk or traverse through a figure.

The fact that teachers do *not* teach listening to tango music (or distinguishing musical timing or phrases), makes the apprentices want to "insert" the basic steps at whatever time, losing all coherence with the structure of the music. That is, by placing the focus on the sequence of basic steps, it will cost us more:

a) Listen to the *beat* (timing).
b) Perceive the beat (every few bars there's an accent).
c) The phrases.
d) The cadence (where there is a closing of one idea and opening of another).

For all this and because it is the opposite of improvising (one of the most interesting values that social tango has) it is not at all advisable to use the famous sequence of "basic steps" as a pedagogical element.

Approach(es)

During the learning process we'll not only work with bodily skills, but also with the ways of learning new things. Challenging current processes is a fundamental part of the coach's work. New brain "wiring," the product of learning, has to be strong enough to face challenges such as:

- Learning to dance the tango.
- Entering a community where social, emotional and bodily skills are required.
- Be prepared to "flow" and enjoy yourself within an (apparently) chaotic and ever-changing environment.
- Strengthen the capacity for perception, intuition, of presence and 360 ° attention.

We assume that those who are at an intermediate or advanced level will know how to ask the coach what they think they need to learn or improve because they already recognize the figures and also have defined standards that let them (to a greater or lesser extent) recognize where *they are* and state where *they want to be* in terms of learning

The coach's work with one or two novice clients

Being a coach for apprentices starting from scratch fills me with honor and happiness. I consider it a huge responsibility and I assume, when they have sufficient tools, that they will be able to continue their learning by choosing their own style with those teachers or schools that provide them with what they deem necessary.

Let me be clear that I personally believe in a rapid process and not to have them as clients forever, basically because when we spend a lot of time together we'll probably share the same "blind spots."

> *My mission is to accompany them during their initial learning*

I consider it essential to provide the opportunity and shed light on the importance of developing their own criteria (and not copying mine, which is what works for me).

Bearing in mind that there are several teaching models, and that I have no idea where they're going to continue learning at the end of our contract, I assume that it's good to be able to use several systems so that they'll have the experience and exposure to the pros and cons of each one.

Before beginning, we will agree to:

- Define goals
- The number or sessions
- The location
- Days and times
- The duration (expressed in minutes)
- The cost
- The method of payment
- The cancellation policy
- The number of participants/coaches
- The clothing and footwear suitable for the activity
- Favorable health condition
- The privacy and confidentiality of the sessions

The ability to coordinate and agree on these factors gives our clients a first impression of us, while they provide the same information to us.

Before starting, always check to see if there are any medical prescriptions or physical limitations. If you have any doubts, you should consult a health professional, first.

At the beginning we will support learning in three complementary channels:

1. Personal Coach: Exclusive and "custom-made" learning opportunity for the client.

2. Homework: Exercises that can be practiced at home, in front of a mirror, to "educate the body." Music to "educate the ear" and videos to develop the principles

3. Group classes: To practice with other dance partners, learning to recognize different signals and personal styles.

During the time contracted by the client, we will start by previewing the framework in which the content will be delivered (and everything that we consider advisable to warn about, such as *what to expect*). Regardless, the surprise factor and flexibility should be part of the coach's art to help, clarify or make the rhythm of the course flow.

Musical framework

Most clients are not accustomed to listening to tango, so learning to do so will be part of the challenge that the coach will propose.

To cause a gradual adjustment process to result, it's a good idea to use a playlist that includes:

a) For warmth and first contacts with tango: *modern tangos*, performed by current orchestras with bass, drums, synthesizer and sounds that are familiar to the apprentice.

b) Gradually move towards a selection of *traditional tangos*. Although we don't focus on the musical aspect during the first physical exercises, our client will begin to register and generate a new relationship with the tango instruments. Week by week, class by class, some tangos will begin to be more "familiar."

c) This musical selection is not about the coach's personal taste, but its goal is to make the client listen to the tangos that are more likely to be recognized in any milonga in the world.

d) During the time where the focus is on music, we can share a story or anecdote related to that tango, thus fixing it much more strongly in the client's memory. Including the photo of the conductor or even a video can be powerful tools for achieving this end.

e) Being able to find tangos that are propitious for demonstrating nuances and different forms of expression. It's time to remove the prejudice of the "melancholic tango" and be able to have the necessary resources for sharing the extraordinary variety of styles, lyrics and energy that the genre has to offer us.

f) Sometimes listening to a very rhythmic tango ("rabid") can distract the client, so it's very healthy to recognize if the tango is *transporting you* or irritating you. Maybe a little silence is what is needed to let the apprentice process the information that we are sharing at a certain moment.

First encounter / Social distances

If communication with the client has been by phone or text but not in person, in our first face-to-face meeting we will be very attentive to his greeting and to the distances that he establishes to converse with us.

Coaches very often assume that we're going to work with embraces and different dynamics that include physical contact with the client. For us, this is something normal and everyday, but we don't yet know what the other thinks about it.

Considering that factor, what we can ask ourselves and him is:

> *What does he say when he declares his desire to dance tango?*

We can consult books on body language and non-verbal communication, or learn from practice and observation about "social" distances and the pre-established spaces that the client brings. Any of them will help us obtain valuable information that allows us to determine a starting point to start working with the person or persons that hire us.

Note "sensitivity"

Working in places where there are works of art (paintings, sculptures or mosaics) I have had the opportunity to experience different "sensitivities" on the part of clients. It is interesting to note if the person, when arriving, has the goal of getting into the action immediately or if, on the other hand, he's interested in what's in the place and empathizes with those present (at least with the coach).

This inspection will serve us as a starting point when we propose working with nuances and details that integrate the perception of music, instruments, space and, above all, your dance partner.

Health

We will always consult the client about his health, counting on his sincerity and good will in this regard. However, it's important for us to make sure that he is in the necessary condition to work out with us in practice. During the "warm-up" with individual exercises, we will have the opportunity to gain a initial record (not definitive) about their performance with respect to the challenges incumbent with certain movements. Then we will regulate and administer the degree of difficulty recommended based on this previous record (which may well change in a few minutes, which is why we "warm up").

Take into account the "comparison"

Working with someone who has never taken dance lessons requires a very different approach compared to the one who did. On the other hand, we will pay attention to whether the person claims to already "know" how to dance the tango.

If the person or persons have never taken any kind of dance classes, they will tend to compare the approach with the ideas about it they come with, like what they've heard or even seen in a movie, but generally the way in which they accept the class is going to represent something new

On the other hand, if the clients have already taken classes or have "their" tango teacher, there is a good chance that everything we say, suggest or show them will be compared with what they've previously experienced or had taught to them. This mechanism is almost automatic; there are those who will even "challenge" our suggestion because it does not fit the one they've learned and, also, those who are not going to challenge us but will accept the information with caution, showing some need to base what we say in contrast to their preconceived ideas.

In order not to suffer (I write *to suffer* in an explicit sense) the whole encounter, a great tool to keep in mind is the objective agreed upon before starting. Always basing our proposal on the basis of what it is for, using indicators to show the effectiveness of the exercise in order to achieve the goal, is a good way to overcome this situation.

Initial rhythm

Both the us and our client, before starting work, were doing something requiring energy and a mental or emotional state other than what we'll need to develop this activity that we're called to.

Because of this, it's very important to keep in mind that in order to be more effective in our communication, we must "tune in" our energies. When we're on the same "frequency," information will flow in both directions.

It doesn't matter that we've just finished meeting with other apprentices, even that we have viewed the same themes. Closing the meetings requires a very different cadence compared with opening the meetings.

Each day, with each client or group of clients, our vibration and relationship will be unique. The moment we want to "standardize" our internal rhythm, we will stop providing a customized service that depends on the person who has placed their trust in us when choosing us.

Sometimes, I have clients who get stressed out over the possibility of being late for the appointment, so the usual Buenos Aires transit can be stressful just before we meet. This makes a pause to adjust very necessary before suggesting any activity after their arrival (breathing, tone of voice and cadence when speaking can be key in this context).

Warm-up

This is a very important time, because both parties are acquiring information from each other; the empathy generated during this stage will condition the rest of the day.

This is where we check their balance, coordination, general rhythm, breathing rhythm, body axis, mood, energy, eye contact, relationship with your body and the surrounding space.

During the warm-up we can use many of the figures that are then going to "label." At this stage his task is to "look and copy" (look at the action of the coach and reproduce it), without thinking or reasoning about it, or getting any explanation. The amount of "difficult" things that people can easily do is impressive, precisely because they don't know "how difficult they are."

> *Present the "warm-up" with simplicity and an attitude of "This is very easy; the hard part will come later."*

This is an extraordinary tool. The good thing is that at the end of this stage, the coaches have been able to check which figures they are capable of doing already and which (as yet) they are not.

"Structure of the embrace" and basic elements

Beginning to improvise movements from this point is very healthy, considering that in the milonga they will have to resolve things quickly when they meet people. It's worth clarifying that improvising and having no fixed structure requires the brain to generate new neural connections to face this challenge. This synapse consumes a lot of energy and it's our responsibility to administer the level of demand so that the apprentice doesn't end up "out of gas" before the end of the agreed time.

> *At this stage, it is appropriate to check the client's relationship with "mistakes," that is, how he or she behaves and what emotional impact he or she has when the planned activity doesn't work out as expected.*

Structures and sequences

These are a set of combined steps or movements that are labeled with a name so that they can be memorized and repeated until they flow out and, if possible, within the musical tempo. This is the most common model in the teaching of tango, where a sequence of figures is used, and the performance is worked on and improved on it.

"Separators"

Between the different stages, actions that I call "separators" are very useful. Below are examples:

- Show some videos of different dance styles.
- Offer them some candy, drink mate tea, etc.
- Show *trailers* of tango movies.
- Point out historical places or notable bars related to tango.
- Share tango anecdotes that make the day more entertaining.
- It's also good to see photographs of some of the directors of tango orchestras, images they will recognize in the milongas in the future.

The separators "oxygenate" the brain and relieves tension generated in the previous stage, preparing us for the next one.

It's good to breathe

Throughout our meeting we'll keep in mind the fact that sometimes the challenge of learning causes us to have a "short" or, say, breathing that is unfavorable for the learning process. Checking our breathing and that of the client is a very useful and simple indicator, which affects practically the whole experience. Reminding yourself to breathe or "intervening" in your own breathing can give the other person an awareness of his.

Note expression

When listening to specific orchestras, the apprentice will have a specific expression. If we can detect where his taste is "going," we will have a great tool to organize our musical playlist according to the objectives we previously agreed upon.

> *I remember a visit to a milonga in Europe. When we arrived, we saw with surprise that people stayed dancing during the "cortina" (in that case a slow international theme of the eighties). It was impressive to see the pleasure on their faces when dancing to a familiar theme that sounded familiar (during the 30 or 40 seconds that the cortina lasted), almost the opposite to the expression of those dancing Argentine tangos recorded in the forties, where the focus was on making "tango" figures and sequences.*

Multimedia

A very useful tool to use is *video captures*. Seeing yourself dancing is already an interesting experience; having *feedback* from the video record allows you to work on specific moments and check the results over time.

Remember the relation to space

One thing to keep in mind is to remind clients that the "space" factor in the milonga is fundamental and conditions their experience. In other words, during private practice with the coach, they (usually) have more space than they will have in a real milonga, in addition to the feeling of movement that all other couples produce dancing around. Include exercises that strengthen this aspect is a valuable resource that clients will appreciate.

Blinking as indicator

There are disciplines that study these patterns. I just want to mention here that the pattern, rhythm of the blink or "the look" of the client provides an extraordinary amount information that, combined with other factors such as music, action, conversation, breathing, etc., can be indicators of fatigue, confusion, a specific emotion and many other things that each coach will know how to decode and take advantage of with practice.

Sense of humor

Being spontaneous about the sense of humor is essential, but first we must check how open the person is to laugh at himself and his "mistakes."

If we have a repertoire of funny jokes or anecdotes along with comments associated with the practice of tango, it's an advantage we can use only if we have great empathy toward the apprentice and the idea that nothing we say is against him/her or is perceived as a value judgment on his person.

Attention and sequential thinking

Sometimes the apprentices want to coordinate the movements with the other person following sequential logic:

Movement A + Movement B = Figure C

However, this logic is not always going to be useful considering that in the previous scheme each item happened at a different time and right after the previous one.

Some tango figures require the movements to be simultaneous and different from what our partner is doing, with specific tension and in a specific time, so that the result is what's expected.

I have witnessed the hard work of recognizing the limitations of this "sequential logic," because many people find it very useful in their daily lives and this fact signifies a revelation to them. It's worth noting that the more they resist, the more difficult it is for learning to be effective.

For this we will facilitate a path using a "watch and copy" resource, meaning, observe and repeat a part of the action without any explanation. At this point in the process, the coach will remain attentive not to let linear thinking be unleashed, leading the apprentice's attention to any irrelevant detail within the action. It seems magical, but simply inviting people to observe something other than "sequential order" means that it's then the client himself who discovers how to do it and who (now) has the capacity to explain it.

Summary of content by levels

In reference to the order of content, I consider it effective to be able to divide them into three different levels, independent of role (leader/*follower*).

1. The first two stages (warm-up and structure of the embrace) are integrated into a puzzle-like format, showing movements or small sequences, single steps or isolated figures with little (or no) explanation

Assuming that human beings tend to seek meaning in things - or order to them - we can let the apprentice to discover for himself how the pieces that were given to him fit together. It's very effective and strengthens his self-esteem, to personally discover how to dance, instead of someone *teaching him* to do it.

Different levels

Level 1:

a) Foot support/weight change

b) Pivot

c) Movement (linear A - B) [coordinate with partner/music]

The first level provides the basis for improvised dance, focusing on the points of support with the floor.

The pivots are on this previously determined point of support and the movement is from point of support A to point of support B. In all cases we work on the ways of communication from the leader and the feedback offered by the *follower*.

Level 2:
      d) Turning code (vs. linear A - B)
      e) Barridas
      f) Sacadas

In the second level we work on how to rotate and how to distinguish the mark of a linear movement [from A to B] from that of the "turn" of the *follower* around the leader (circular). Then the "barridas" and "sacadas," like illusions that are seen in the feet of the dancers, are the product of effective communication in the upper part of their bodies.

Level 3:
      g) Free leg
      h) Colgadas (off axis)
      i) Volcadas (off axis)

In the third level we will focus on the free leg and the *off-axis,* called "colgadas" and "volcadas."

The reason for putting the most striking figures last is that I think they distract the apprentices before their improvisation skills are strengthened. In this order it's harder to want to already make figures that can be repeated (without the mental effort that is required to improvise).

The three consciousnesses

Whether in *workshops* or individual sessions, I have been finding different concepts on which we can work, investigate and "open" conversations. These concepts can range from the most superficial to whatever depth that participants wish to grant. It is wonderful to witness the *insights* that some people experience as a product of the analysis of these three levels of consciousness. Here we have them in separate order, but the extraordinary thing is that these consciousnesses work simultaneously.

Speaking *in terms of tango* gives us the possibility of working on aspects that are reflected in everyday life.

Below is a list of my own reflections, based on my experience in both individual work and with groups of people. This list is only as an example and as a personal opinion. My wish is that everyone will have their own list.

Self awareness

- ## Opposite energies/tension

Being aware of our muscle tone and the tension necessary to signal or perceive the signal is essential. This tension is internal and is the result of energies that go in opposite directions (up/down, forward/backward). A common image is to think of the lower body pushing towards the floor while from the waist up we extend an upward pressure. Our stomach is "exposed" and our rib cage is present as the center and source of the information from which we will coordinate with our dance partner.

- ## Embellishments

Embellishments can happen on our way from a point A to a point B, or when we are at a fixed point or "stop." The challenge is for them to happen without affecting the communication between the dancers. Through them we can express our "reading" of the music, of the moment or our mood.

- ## Limits (own)/Energy budget

In dancing a tanda, we're going to be aware of having an energy budget for everything that implies coordination with our partner. Sometimes we meet people who seem to need to be "pushed" to move, or that "hang" on your arm. In those cases, being aware of how much energy you're willing to invest prevents you from finding yourself struggle or taking charge of "making your partner dance."

We are not to push anyone (or to be pushed). Each one is responsible for having the necessary energy to move their own weight from point A to point B.

> ### *When I dance the tango,*
> ### *what are my limits?*

- ## Motivation

What for am I going to tango? What's the benefit? Where do I feel it or do I perceive it? How much do I want to dance? In which orchestras do I find a greater stimulus? How does my life change when tango dancing?

- ## Body/body axis/balance

Where does my body start and where does it end? How far will my foot go when I take the next step? Tension? Where do I look when I dance? How much influence does the position of the hip and its relationship with the torso have? Does my body axis affect the way I dance or say something about me? Do I have balance? What is balance and how do I interpret it? How do I know I'm tired?

- Emotion

Dancing with a defined emotion or recognizing the emotions that are triggered in me by tango dancing is a fundamental value. A genuine and conscious emotion impacts on the whole experience.

When I dance the tango, what emotions do I experience? Where do I feel them? Do I have a body testimony? With what state of mind am I going to milonguear? What mood do I return to?

- Style/personal taste/criteria/rituals

Throughout time and different periods in the evolution of tango, different types of styles and criteria have been developed, not only concerning the dance but also other aspects, such as the "taste" of the tango DJ, the embellishments, types of embrace, milongueros codes, way of stepping, body lines, costumes, use of space and other rituals.

It is very important to keep this in mind when visiting a milonga or practice for the first time. Being aware of the style we choose as our own will allow us to prefer places, experiences and people that correspond to our style or taste.

- ## What do I hear?

You do not have to be an expert connoisseur of orchestras; it's just a matter of perception, of being sensitive ton each session's music and the way you want to interpret it when dancing. Their order (and the energy that each one "moves") is sometimes favorable and is compensated by our own tempo. For example, if I just danced a "rabid and choppy" session, I may want a more calm and relaxing one for the next one.

> *Sometimes the DJ's criteria coincide with ours; other times it doesn't.*

Who I choose to dance with for each tanda is also essential. There are people with whom it is very enjoyable to dance to a certain rhythm and cadence but during another orchestra or musical tempo you do not enjoy yourself as much (or you suffer!).

- ## How do I judge the other?

Knowing what factors I value when judging how someone dances is something that is not taught but must be learned. Being conscious of choosing someone with whom I relate is a determining factor in the milonguero's experience.

- What do I feel when I embrace?

As time passes, our criteria evolve with us. It is interesting to pay attention to what I feel when embracing and what defines a "good embrace" *for me*. What determines a good embrace has to do with me perceiving the other and my own standards to recognize and value it. Almost as a general rule, we can agree that being aware of the moment of creating the embrace on the floor is an instance of a sublime, sacred and timeless encounter.

Those who grab one another to charge off on a few steps miss one of the most extraordinary treasures that tango has given us.

That treasure is *finding ourselves*, to be in the present where the expectation that we had at the moment of the invitation materializes, that risk that implies that it may not feel as we expected or that it is unparalleled and we wish it would never end.

Sometimes I think that "there" is where that first kiss is hidden that we once gave, or where all our "first times" hidden.

He who ruins that moment in pursuit of the steps to come, has lost something that is not recovered. That moment is unique, we can redo it but each redo is different because I am being different and my partner also.

As I was learning to dance the tango, I also learned to embrace as if it were "the first time," to feel the fear and insecurity of a teenager and irresponsibility for the future, so as not to miss that present moment.

- Am I aware of having chosen to be here?

Sometimes I think that learning to dance the tango and living it as an experience that enriches us requires paying a price, a price nobody warned us about. When we're going to learn to box, for example, we know in advance that we'll take some punches (in the hope of learning to give some). So, in addition to paying the gym, we budgeted for some ice bars to take the bruises down. However, in my opinion, in tango this common sense is not as clear.

We each are come to tango for very different reasons, but we agree in a moment of innocence and naivety that, seen from a distance, puts us on a plane almost equal to the one we live in when we first reach kindergarten. To learn, not only do you need to pay for the lessons, you also have to take them and receive the stomps (and give them). They also challenge us, since some "teachers" have little didactics and even less patience.

> *Sometimes we find ourselves practicing with a stranger who tells us that all we do is wrong (he is rarely right).*
>
> *After this, some return home with their morale on the floor (they told me, it never happened to me, and I hope it never happens to me again).*
>
> *When I finally get "the baby step" with this partner, the teacher says that you have to change your partner. Why? Ugh, start over!*
>
> *Finish the class and tell us to dance ... How can I dance if they hit me everywhere? (well, I collided, too), my feet hurt and I forgot the step ... The second person with whom I danced had the same perfume as my ex ... The third one was soaked in perspiration, am I the only one that I feels that way? How did I get into this situation?*

- Silence?

You notice the difference in roles here, except in the perception of silence itself. I mean that when we stand one or more seconds while the tango is being executed (and we still hold the embrace), that moment has great value because it shows that we are there, embracing, sensing and feeling, very close, to the point that sometimes we no longer clearly distinguish our limits.

One conclusion I reached is that the "quality of the silences" is a reflection and extraordinary *feedback* on the quality of the relationship of the couple at that moment (although they are new to each other). Normally we can fill time together, with actions or embellishments, but silence ... only fills up "being."

> *I don't know if you can lie, but I like to believe that I do not.*

With respect to the roles, when we speak of the "leader," the one who "signals," etc., it reveals his appreciation of silence and his generosity in sharing this time of expression. In other words, the leader can decide when to stop (it's better to be consistent with the music), but also offering his partner time to choose how to express herself, to close a musical phrase or simply to stay in place.

In tango we do not have to step at all times; the important thing is the awareness of wanting to continue it... or to stop.

- Identification in doing (*feedback*)

Being aware of how well we identify when what we're doing makes it possible to recognize the risk that it signifies.

When we're dancing or learning, we can receive opinions or criticism about our activity and we sometimes end up defending ourselves as if it were a personal attack, or trying to justify an action as if its value depended on our defense. Or, even worse, is when the other person identifies us with what we are doing. For example: "Bad dancer" or "You don't know what you're doing."

Knowing how well we're willing to accept *feedback* (and who we're willing to accept it from) is a reflection worth making before starting the practice.

Being able to separate our identity from our actions and evaluate them based on effectiveness is a good way to implement it. If we exchange opinions about actions, we will have a neutral learning ground without getting emotionally involved in a way that we don't want.

- Confidence: What do I need to have it? Where do I perceive it?

Trusting in our abilities to dance the tango is fundamental, since this emotion "tints" and conditions all the action, thought and the way in which we judge what we perceive. So:

What's necessary to feel confident?

More than giving an answer, this question suggests that we can consciously develop the process of our own confidence, consider how we feel it and what we recognize that the body registers.

- Wardrobe

Being aware of the wardrobe that favors us is an important detail not only from the aesthetic, but what really makes us feel comfortable in the different moments that are experienced on a milonguera day.

What does this wardrobe tell me about myself?

Awareness of the other person

- Look into the eyes

The gaze is a very important part of our communication and is full of flavoring and characteristics that go beyond the analysis of this book. I simply want to mention that when facing "the other person," we will become aware of all the rest of our body perception and the rest of the senses. When we look each other in the eyes we can transport ourselves to a unique dimension where nothing else matters anymore. Let's be aware that visual contact during the dance gives us *feedback* that strengthens communication or perhaps, on the contrary, distracts us.

> *Sometimes I have the good fortune to witness couples who, when they look into each other's eyes, "disconnect" from the entire environment and remain hypnotized in a dimension of love. For my part, I only have to sigh and wait for the "eclipse" to pass to be able to continue with the activity that has called us.*

> *Other times I see looks that look like "flames" and announce the arrival of a storm...*

- Opposing energy/Resistance - tension/Energy budget

With "the other person," opposing energy must be compensated for with ours, if we want to keep our balance while dancing and coordinating our communication through body perception.

Depending on the style we are dancing, there may be some variant, but almost as a rule, the center of our chest will be a faithful reference as a source of communication between the two bodies. In any case, the rationality of the arms when forming and sustaining *the embrace* also gives us valuable information. For this information to "travel" between the two, "tension" is needed.

> *I always like to remember the "telephone" we made with two tomato cans and a thread that joined them (I only mention this with people of my generation). If the thread wasn't tight, we couldn't hear what the other was saying at the distance that separated us.*

On the other hand, we have an energy budget, whether we are aware of it or not (when we are tired it becomes easier for us to be aware). That amount of energy will be distributed over the time we're going to dance and with the number of people with whom we want to do it. Either to "signal" or to receive "the signal," each person invests a quantity of energy that isn't always the same.

There are those who "hang" on us, who push us and who want to be pushed. In all cases, it is worth saying that "the signal" (like words) is a stimulus that serves us in communicating. When we don't understand each other (or discuss things), we tend to raise our voices or shout, as if that would make the message more effective (it seems that sometimes it does). When dancing, the challenge is to find the minimum energy per message to communicate, but each person is responsible for moving their own body from point A to point B.

> *Some people like to push, or be pushed, shout or be shouted at, but in all cases it's a matter of knowing whether or not we want to invest that energy in that conversation.*

In my particular case, it was very revealing to begin to be aware of my responsibilities and to know where the energy limit that I was going to put into each session (as in a conversation) was.

- Time and space for embellishments

When and how to embellish is at the discretion of each dancer, and it's worth saying that each person can embellish on their own at different moments of the dance, but the leader is the one who has the prospect of facilitating and offering greater opportunities to the *follower*.

Recognizing a dance partner who "listens" not only to the music but also to the tempo, who perceives the desire and the will to express herself through embellishments is very important. The generosity of the leader in respecting these moments is very valuable and it's good to be able to discover this in advance.

Each personality is expressed in the form of embellishments, moods and energy (of that moment) as well. We won't always coincide in all these factors at the same time, so we must be careful with our expectations regarding the encounter with our partner.

- Limits (explicit and virtual)

With respect to "the other person," we have different levels or ways of perceiving the limits. Let's first talk about the explicit, which we can define as our height, weight and body volume. These and many other factors determine opportunities and also limits. And with respect to our colleagues too, by being aware of mine, I can now analyze them in relation to the other.

> *For example, if I am very tall and choose to dance a tanda with a very short partner, I have to be aware of what position, embrace or style will allow us to better coordinate the dance. It seems an obvious concept but it is common to hear of certain people who were "victims" of the "imposed" style, as if the other person could voluntarily grow twenty centimeters taller for the dance.*

On the other hand, there are limits in the embrace since the leader will propose an embrace more or less open according to several factors, one of which is the space available on the dance floor, because when there are too many couples dancing we have less space to create certain figures or walks. It is the responsibility of the leader to offer a safe dance space (at the least) within the embrace.

With respect to the virtual limits, I am referring to factors that are not explicit, such as, for example, what I think my partner may or may not be able to propose to me, and whether they are figures (leader) or embellishments/variants (*follower*).

Another virtual limit has to do with my internal conversation about my partner. If I like this person a lot I sometimes feel conditioned in my actions so as not to show any evidence in my actions that there are those who are "clumsy" in the simplest things. Another variant is about contact; some students raise the issue of not knowing "where to touch." In general, this suggests that they are focusing on "that" particular issue.

In every case, an important resource is to be aware of that way of seeing the other, of accepting and of being sincere in our intention. If I really want to dance with you, I will focus on the dance, on flow and enjoy the whole scene, while if I'm thinking about *whether to put my hand higher or lower*, that's very noticeable and generates great discomfort for both. If you cannot deal with this situation it's advisable to first resolve it in your own head before inviting or accepting an invitation. You can also tell yourself another story about it, one that allows you to enjoy it and especially not invade or inconvenience other people.

- The body of the other person: support points/axes/size/height

Depending on the music and the partner, we will prefer different types of embraces. Recognizing the importance of "body axes" and how they work during the dance, long before accepting or inviting someone to dance, is a good idea.

We call the imaginary axes that we can trace on the human body: *body axes*.

Axis N ° 1 (vertical): Imaginary straight line that goes from the point of support on the floor to the highest point of the head.

Axis N° 2 (horizontal): Line that we can draw between the edges of the shoulders.

Axis N° 3 (horizontal): Straight line between the edges of each side of the hips.

The points of support between the dancers, the style of dance and the space that we have on the floor will vary according to the body dimensions of each one.

- Balance

When we are already (quite) aware of our own balance, we will become aware of our partner's balance and how much it affects us, i.e., this is a very valuable point of consciousness because it can change for several reasons. In general our balance will reflect in real time "how balanced" we are and it is a very valuable feedback to recognize if we are tired or have excess energy, if we have had too much alcohol or even if our level of concentration is adequate for dancing.

- ## Agree on the hug

There are those who "already have" an embrace, and it is "that" for everything (even for life). But some of us have several embraces and we count on them to relate to each other in a certain way or to express ourselves with respect to music. Each embrace offers us different possibilities (and limits) and having several options gives us flexibility to balance the energies that will be exchanged with our partners.

- ## Honesty/Consistency

With few exceptions, the other person is neither a mentalist nor knows how to read thoughts. However, those of us who dance the tango begin to develop a perception through dancing that allows us to detect a "noise" in communication, an interference as in a badly tuned radio in which two conversations are heard at the same time. Lying when dancing is very difficult (I like to believe that it is impossible) because while we don't lie or hide with words, which we are more accustomed to, we try with our body to do something very complex, dancing, which usually leaves us exposed to the incoherence of our intentions and our actions.

Therefore, be aware of: "What am I saying about the other person?" (What internal conversation am I have with myself about the other person) and "What do I think of him or her?" This is fundamental. It seems obvious and common sense, but sometimes in order to dance we make the mistake of doing it no matter what with anyone and in any circumstance. It's not just about me, here, but I'm involving another person, which is also good to recognize.

- Cabeceo

The cabeceo is a milonguero ritual par excellence, which many apprentices reject and find great difficulty in practicing. It consists of a first visual contact with the person with whom we wish to dance.

To cite an example, in the case Man-leader/Woman-*follower* the woman looks into the eyes of the dancer with whom she wishes to dance letting him know that she is willing to dance this tanda with him. When the dancer meets her gaze (if he also wants to dance that tanda with her), he makes a small movement of his head that we call "cabeceo." Once he has executed the movement, she will accept with a slight movement, as if nodding, or declining, lowering or running her eyes to another place (if she changed her mind).

Normally we leaders like to think that the pitch begins with us, that we "choose," but, in my opinion, the follower *is the first to determine if we are going to meet their willing gaze or not. Then, the second comes from our nod and third from acceptance (as a counter test).*

It is worth saying that all this ritual takes place "at a distance," for whether great or small, there is a distance between both parties.

From my point of view the cabeceo has a list of advantages and disadvantages, of which I will list a few:

Advantages

* It saves the pride of the one who makes the invitation, because if I get up from my table and go directly to the person I am going to invite and in front of all the other people my invitation is rejected, everyone can see me. Nobody likes to be rejected, let alone in public.

* It's not invasive with respect to who receives the invitation, like when the one approaching a table to make an invitation invites a commitment (public) from the other person, either to accept (a

commitment) or decline the invitation, the latter of which some people may not want to go through, refraining from invite her or him to dance. On the other hand, the fact that someone doesn't accept dancing this tanda with me doesn't mean that she won't be willing to accept in future tandas.

Disadvantages

* People with visual problems may get confused about the invitation. Some milongas are full of people and several people are sitting next to each other, which makes it difficult to identify to whom the invitation is addressed. In the same way, the one who is going to cabeceo has a great challenge making his intention towards the right person noticed.

* There are people who have a hard time making eye contact with others (the gaze of a milonguero/ra is very special and an experience in itself).
* There are other people who don't like to "offer" themselves to dance and prefer that some comes explicitly to ask them, as is often the case in other places of social activity.

- Embrace

Being able to recognize the orchestras and the styles of each one lets us to choose how to express ourselves through dance. Walking together at the beginning is already an achievement; then we start walking together in time and then we even have the chance to "get out" of the intense tempo and choose when to return. Having several styles of embrace to offer or an embrace flexible enough to adapt to the different rhythms and tempos of tango is a valuable virtue for enjoying this experience.

- Preserve the pride of the other person (beware of your identification with performing/dancing)

If they ask for *feedback*, it's good to talk about the action and not about the person. If that is clear, even if we don't agree, our relationship will not be compromised.

- Empathy/Respect

Being aware of how important it is to empathize with the other is fundamental, because the foundations that we started to build from the first glance we shared, or the first words we exchanged, will condition the way in which the relationship goes. Some have said that there's no second chance to make a good first impression. I think that letting the other person know our good will, that what "we say" about him/her is good and positive, builds the relationship.

- Space for mistakes or silliness

Sometimes we find the permeability and openness of mind in the other person to try new things, to innovate, to make mistakes even at the risk of appearing ridiculous. It doesn't always happen nor is always us who offers that space to the other.

> *Many times I see people dancing with the typical "serious tango face" expression or "the tango look." They are taking themselves and their dance very seriously, often dancing milongas or the funniest tangos that exist. At first glance, and without knowing anything about tango, you can appreciate the paradoxical and ridiculous situation.*

Being aware of the "virtual" space for error opens up a range of possibilities that are worth taking advantage of.

• Overcoming differences (physical, cultural, language)

I like to think of tango as a language, and I'm passionate about meeting people from all over the world who *speak* that language. As in the Spanish or English languages, there are variants, but we have a number of "words" in common that allow us to coordinate our actions.

When we find ourselves dancing the tango, we prefer to focus on what we have in common, on our best intentions of finding the best points of contact to be able to flow together. If we make the mistake of focusing on our differences, we will probably lose the richness that arises from the unique combination of amalgamating all "the distinctives" in our common points.

- "Listen" to the body of the other person/Ask with your body

Being aware of the body of your partner, what's comfortable, her limits and her timing provides us with deeper communication, where words do not mediate but which we interpret as we perceive it from the body of the other, at the same time as we offer stimulus so that our partner can also interpret it.

> *I remember sometimes dancing with an experienced milonguera, who apparently was not very happy following my signals out of tempo (I didn't even know I was out of time). The thing is that little by little, with subtle resistance, she managed to "ask" me to slow down my tempo for a fraction of a second so that the steps coincided with the beat of the music... a true teacher. Without saying a word, everything was said.*

The same happens with respect to spaces; there are figures in which we need more space in the embrace, and the other person is not aware of that. So having the ability to ask for space or shrink the space is a great tool that we should keep in mind for our milongueras outings.

How conscious am I of my personal space? Can I ask for more space? Under what circumstances? What defines my space? What defines the other person's space?

• Excess energy (directing / channeling)

Sometimes we feel an excess of energy that isn't flowing. It's very useful to recognize that the way we walk and the energy that we "send" to the floor is something personal. Regardless of the role (leader or *follower*), we can tread with more or less energy, making sure that the rest of energy doesn't have to be absorbed by (going through) our partner. Or, channel it through the embellishments.

Our breathing is also a great channel through which our energies can flow and balance themselves in relation to those of our dance partners.

- My performance vs. Us (am I disheveled?)

If I am more concerned about my performance than *our* dancing, I will miss one of the wonders of tango. Resigning our individuality in pursuit of being "one" sounds esoteric, but those who have danced for a while can attest to the issue.

> *If I think about my hairstyle while I'm making love, something is wrong. The same applies when dancing social tango.*

- Surprise and be surprised

Regardless of the role, it is very pleasant to be able to surprise your partner and/or be surprised. The embellishments, ways of stepping, of embracing, the emotion when breathing and many other factors cause us to find something new during (even) an ordinary figure. Breaking the routine, changing patterns, energies and moods make the same couple become "different" from one tanda to another and the experience is similar but never identical to the previous one. It doesn't happen to us all, but if we are attentive in dancing the tango, we'll pass through unique moments.

- Genuine desire to embrace the other

Sometimes "we put the cart in front of the horse" and we lose consciousness of embracing another human being, with all that that means.

If we think about the figures, ourselves or how others see us, we forget about who we have in our arms and we're going to commit a regrettable mistake. When I invite you to dance or I accept your invitation, at that moment we must coincide with a genuine desire to embrace each other; if I have any doubts about it, it will show itself during the dance or at the very moment of finding ourselves in the embrace.

As we said before, it is very difficult to lie with our body: there are too many indicators that act all at the same time. On the other hand, when the value is supported by what happens between our plexus instead of our feet, we will be able to transcend the obstacles with greater fluidity.

- When does "I" come before "we?"

We live our lives with the well-known "to do list," things we "must" do and check to ensure they going properly.

To dance the tango "we" must follow certain rules and there is a list of things to check, but the "we" is in first place.

When I have a genuine desire to communicate through an embrace, all the lists clear; it's not necessary to check them; they appear and check themselves.

> *In this book I invite you to be aware of many details, but if you focus only on the "we," everything else will fall in place in due time.*

- ## Jealousy?

In the present work we're talking about a social dance, and therefore the focus is not only on learning to dance the tango, but also on being able to go to the milongas and dance with different people. You could ask yourself:

- Why am I going to a milonga?
- What role do I give to tango in my life and my relationships?
- What is jealousy?
- When do I feel jealous?
- Where do you feel (body testimony)?
- With respect to who?
- Do I think something "should" be different?
- Am I making any comparisons?
- Is there something or someone that I consider my "own" or "exclusive"?

Asking myself questions can be a way to check my beliefs about it and what's grabbing my attention when I feel jealous. What causes us jealousy with tango is a very interesting field of reflection.

- Wardrobe

When meeting another person, our wardrobe has to be comfortable not only for us individually. The other person is going to embrace us, so we'll have points of contact and it's important not to have surprises once on the dance floor.

One factor is the texture of the garments. We will be embracing and coordinating movements for about ten minutes; there are garments that in supporting the hand for ten minutes are very uncomfortable, with textures, holes, and metal decorations (which can even hurt a partner).

When choosing clothing, it's very useful to "budget" how much skin is going to be exposed and the risk that some parts of our body will be exposed, which can generate an uncomfortable situation for both parties.

One question to keep in mind is: *Why do we dress ourselves?*

How we interact with the environment

- Recognize the "rhythm and flow" of the crowd

Each milonga has its atmosphere, a way to flow, which is determined by several factors but many of us will agree that the organizer is the one that invites a certain group of people with certain characteristics and energies.

When arriving at a milonga or practice, it's fundamental to take the time to check that rhythm, if it has something to do with us, and decide if we really want to participate. If we could watch the milongas from "the next floor," we would observe something similar to the flow of water. There are places where it looks like a lake, almost uniform and may even seem like there's no movement, with all couples flowing in harmony with each other, with the music, turning in unison and progressing counterclockwise (as is proper). In others we see one of those fast rivers where kayaking is practiced; it seems like an adventure to participate and leave unscathed from the rolling of stilettos, boleos, confusing directions and the irregularity of the energy. Within these extremes there is a whole range of options, so being aware of this will avoid many misunderstandings and contradictory feelings.

- Palate or taste of the DJ

To recognize it it's not necessary to be a historian, to know the years of the recording or to have a tattoo that says "tango." You just have to want to be aware of it and to pay a little attention. Recognizing the energy generated by a tanda, not only in my partner and I, but also in the public, lets me evaluate whether or not the DJ is connected to what is happening on the dance floor.

Tango has a wide spectrum of recordings and styles that range from the quietest to the most energetic. As a general rule, I think that any excess is bad and if the DJ has a *playlist* that he's put together before leaving home, there's a good chance that one of the tandas will discourage the dancers from continuing to dance.

Others have no idea even of the selection of tangos that they did in the same tanda, which means that we're going to discover surprises (they may be good) but, by definition, if I invited a partner to dance a "romantic" tanda, I would prefer not to encounter a different rhythm during the same tanda.

- Rules of the venue (written and unwritten) / Rituals

There are "traditional" milongas with written rules, literally and explicitly placed in the entrance. If you don't follow these rules, you will have to go dancing somewhere else. There are also milongas with unwritten rules but known by everybody. Everybody?

From there to the most chaotic milongas imaginable, the range is wide. The most flexible are called "practices." At any rate, for those of us who are already in the environment, we take for granted a number of details that the newcomer will suffer in ignorance of. More than writing a list, I prefer to invite you to be aware that all milongas or practices have some pattern, some unwritten rule, rituals, and ways that govern them, from being able to do or not do boleos, practice a figure or keep talking on the dance floor.

Knowing how far the "freedom" goes is information that should be aware of in advance (or as soon as possible) so as not to find ourselves off side *saying "Weren't we allowed to do what we wanted?"*

- Groups / Alpha Leaders / Idols

As in any other social space in which we will participate, in the milonga we will find idols, macho men and/or alpha females, life partners or people who exercise some kind of leadership. Their area of influence can be with the people grouped around a table or with almost all those attending the milonga. It is not a trivial fact to know who exercises that role when we're new or newcomers.

> *For most milonguero that I train, when he arrives at another milonga he must have the common sense (not always so common) to check out the leadership. There are some "leaders" who don't need to let you know the role they embody, but there are others who may perceive a threat to their position until they know you or "they get your number."*

Sometimes it's a matter of tact, and maybe inviting the top dog's girlfriend to dance on your first tanda could be seen as a provocation. Yes, I know that it should be the other guy's problem, that if he's so sensitive it's his problem, etc. But no, if I'm the new guy, trying to integrate myself into a community of people that is already in existence before my arrival, I think it will always be better to respect the goodwill of the attendants so they can rest assured that I came to dance and not to steal the show.

- Space

The space that we use to dance corresponds to the total of the milonga/practice audience. We can use more or less space, but if our intention is to integrate we will keep in mind how much space we're going to occupy. At this point, we're already aware of the space we need, how much space is most appropriate to dance with my partner and then about what portion of the dance floor we will need to enjoy ourselves without interrupting the energy flow, not bothering or being bothered by other couples.

- Cabeceo (2nd option)

The cabeceo, in relation to the environment, allows us to make the process of choosing and being chosen (or rejected) more fluid and less exposed. For example, if I explicitly invite a lady and she tells me no, it's not a good idea to invite the lady next to her who just witnessed the whole event.

> *Nobody likes to be "second choice" or chosen "by elimination."*

Therefore, taking into account this detail and using the "cabeceo" will allow us (in case they decline our invitation) to continue looking for a partner without leaving or being obvious to anyone.

- Tandas

By definition, each tanda consists of four tangos, separated from the next by music that we do not dance called a "cortina." The tandas, with some exceptions (such as *Ronda de Ases*), usually have a common criterion, a rhythm, a "color" or an emotion that is shared among the tangos that make it up.

The choice of tangos by the DJ should have a criterion that the dancer can establish during the first stages of the first tango before inviting or accepting the invitation to dance. We want to find people with whom we will enjoy dancing certain tandas, but not others.

There are practices that are not divided into tandas, but such, if we pay attention, that there are four tangos with a "profile," followed by four other tangos from a different one. There are also places that only use tangos downloaded from the Internet, without any apparent thread (I say "apparent" because the playlist can be in alphabetical order or by track number, which is horrid).

On a lighter note, I had the opportunity to go to open "practices" where the list had the same tango twice and nobody noticed. Or a full tanda was repeated and nobody acknowledged remembering either. I even remember one where, during the whole night, there was not a single tango of the "Bandoneón Mayor de Buenos Aires..." I was apparently the only "out of place" person who expected that. This is not a matter of being a fanatic, but, drawing a parallel with football, if we're going to watch a game in Argentina and our number 10 isn't there, we're going to ask ourselves why he's not playing. This is not a question of taste; it's almost impossible to ignore it because of its presence or absence.

In short, there are romantic, moving, choppy, elegant, in a row, plus other multiple descriptions. The point here is to become aware of the value of knowing the mood of yourself, your partner, the public and the one suggested by the DJ.

When all these factors are aligned, a unique experience takes place.

- Wardrobe

There are more formal and more informal milongas.

> *Informal, for that matter, is much the same, because if you go to an "informal" milonga dressed in snappy clothes, you'll be as off-base as you would be in a traditional milonga in flip flops.*

Our wardrobe communicates, whether we like it or not. Perhaps a better way to say it is that others take your image as information they then process to judge you or form an opinion. But beyond that, it's good to be aware that we're going to a public place and that, to have a good experience, we'll have to choose and be chosen, whether to dance, take tango lessons or share a glass of wine while others dance.

- Recognize potential dance partners / Initial judgment / Fundamentals

When we arrive at a place, whatever it is, we look around and express an opinion not only about the place and its (physical) attributes but also about the people and their mood (good vibes), or what we might call "atmosphere."

When we arrive at a milonga it's no different. We look around and judge an impressive number of aspects in a few seconds

Things like the cleanliness of the place, the style and good taste, the age of the people who frequent it, the social conditions, costumes, temperature (does it have air conditioning?), the food, the tablecloths, the lighting, the space, the duration, the ones I like, those I do not, the style of dancing, the unwritten rules, the kind of embrace ("open" or milonguero hug).

Our opinions are based on standards, which we sometimes take for granted. In the case of dancing with others, we'll choose who to dance with either when inviting or when invited. In any case, before accepting or declining an option, we are weighing some of the factors. Which are?

It's not my plan to answer this question, but it's essential to focus and give light to the importance of this process, since many (many!) times I meet people who had some very unpleasant experiences in their encounter with others and in a lot of cases they are presented:

a) As victims.
b) As those who don't understand what's wrong with themselves.

In both cases, the issue is how they assess the way they relate to other milongueros or local people. It's worth remembering that if we're in a train station, in a nightclub or at a demonstration, we are careful who we stay close to and who we prefer to keep at a certain distance (because we interpret them to represent a risk for us). In the milonga, the risk is normally "emotional." If we're not attentive, we can end the night crying because our self-esteem is on the floor.

In the tango community there are people of all kinds. We're not "all good and kind;" therefore know how to evaluate who you're going to talk with, emotion, timing, hugs and even fluids (don't think badly; in summer we sweat enough) is a fundamental factor for going through the experience in a healthy and enriching way.

There are those who say about a certain milonguero that "he danced four years ago," as if that standard was enough evidence to guarantee a good dance or, more importantly, a good interaction with us and the environment.

To continue with this example, I know gentlemen who have been dancing very badly for many years and are unkind to their classmates.

As it happens, the tango is generous and introduces new partners (literally new/beginners) as an inexhaustible source of people on which to demonstrate their "experience" in the matter and make them feel inferior.

Knowing how to judge in advance and recognize these types of characters is an incalculable value on which we must focus and be very aware, since ultimately we're the ones who will accept or will not interact with them.

Sometimes it is not a matter of "dancing well" or "knowing a lot" but of empathy, kindness, generosity in the embrace and an infinite list that everyone can complete to their liking.

Those who start out in tango and take their first steps (within the social environment we call milonga) often encounter self-determined "authorities," having been contemporaries of the days of the greats, or for knowing some pieces by heart.

The issue is the mere fact of having survived "the greats" of that time - I wonder: Which one? It neither makes them great nor contemporaries.

It is not my intention to define what or who is great (or what that means), but to focus on the validation that is sometimes given to certain individuals who add no good energy in the milonga or good experiences in the early stages of the apprentices.

It's very useful to ask ourselves while we watch them dance:

- Do they smile? Do you both smile?
- During the cortinas, does your conversation seem pleasant?
- Is their expression one of enjoyment?
- Do I really want to embrace this person?
- What energy do they have?
- Am I willing to receive *feedback* or do I just want to dance?
- If I have already seen this person criticizing or giving *feedback* on the dance floor, what makes me think that he's not going to try that with me?

On the other hand, taking time before "dashing" to the floor with the first person that crosses your path is a good way to meet the dancers present, see them in action and, depending on that, choose who you're willing to dance with in the next tandas.

- Take the necessary time

Knowing that we are not obliged to dance all the tandas gives us an opportunity to rest, "stop the ball" and enjoy the whole experience, which is not limited exclusively to what happens on the dance floor.

- Group classes before the milonga

For many who have just started, taking a group tango class before the milonga (and in the same place) presents an incomparable and often underestimated advantage.

When we begin in tango, we have no idea of the challenges that we're going to face on our path as apprentices. An implicit challenge is that beyond the "learned" figures and steps, what we're learning is to relate to strangers in a neutral space where (we suppose) we have the same level of learning.

By taking a group class before the milonga, we are gaining experience in meeting people with whom we can practice and improve on what the instructor has explained to us. Greater practice will mean experience and a foundation for the questions we'll ask the instructors in the next class.

Another advantage is that we begin to feel a sense of belonging, knowing (at least by sight) certain people and some recognize us. We begin to share a story, our "beginnings." It's not that we are or will be friends, but somehow we belong to the same "generation."

- Friendly with beginners?

Following the line of the previous chapter, almost by definition milongas which have beginner classes before starting are "friendly" with those who are just beginning. They expect that after the class, some (with courage) will stay to practice what they've learned.
Other milongas are the opposite, and explicitly express their disapproval with having a beginner on the dance floor. The ways to let him know that he's not welcome are multiple and range from the subtle to the most direct, asking him to leave.

It is the task of the instructors to warn their students, in order to avoid having a bad time in public.

We can make a comparison to football, where the limits and spaces are clear. There's almost no way that paying for a ticket gets me on the field with the starting players to play the game. In a milonga, without realizing it, we can find ourselves on a floor full of "professionals" or "tango stars" where we're not welcome.

- Dancers who "listen" vs. "making fancy footwork"

Regardless of the level you're at, it's valuable to be able to recognize the "leaders who listen" (tango) versus "make fancy steps" (those focused on making steps and figures, one after the other). In the case of *followers* it is also important, since her personality will be reflected in the form of "dancing the silences" (enjoying them and not suffering through them), their cadence, way of stepping and balanced ability to embellish during the dance. Taking into account the extraordinary value of "silences" (not of the music, but "silence of movement"), we can conclude that to take a step, suggest a figure or embellish, there must be an emotion in the form of a source of energy that inspires that movement, making it unique to those circumstances.

I was recently in a milonga and I witnessed something that is quite recurrent. A milonguero (social dancer) invited a professional dancer who was in the place to dance. She accepted the invitation and they embraced to dance. From that moment, the behavior of the milonguero could be compared to having an opportunity to drive a Formula 1 car, trying to do all the pirouettes and audacious figures that he thinks he is capable of doing, all without registering even for a moment the expression nor the desire of his partner to be involved in such exhibitionism... Let's be careful who we want to impress, especially if we are "leaders."

- Food

It always seems advisable to eat at a milonga. I think that buying a ticket isn't enough to keep the "wheel" moving. In my opinion, few organizers understand the business from a sustainable perspective over time, providing a service with business criteria. The reality of having a reserved table and having dinner in the place, or at least having a drink, supports the service of waiters, waitresses, cooks and people who tend the bar. It helps to pay the taxes for the place and (it would be good if) it leaves some profit to the one who organized and promoted the milonga.

- Reservations/Table

I like to think of a milonga like chess. The "geographical" position in space influences the game of the milonga. Depending on the table or place that "we get" (or choose), we'll have different opportunities that open. Whether for the cebeceo or for ease of movement when walking around, it's crucial to know the role played by the location.

It is worth mentioning that those who frequent a milonga have already won/reserved their locations or spaces. So let's analyze where it's best for us to sit while we're not dancing.

On the other hand, having a reservation allows you to have a certain place to return to and to always have free, since there will always be people to share with, but it's good to reserve the right to be able to choose who to invite to share your table.

> *Sometimes, during the tanda, we can experience some circumstance that we see as unhappy and for which we change our mood or frame of mind (I was told, since it never happened to me, it's never going to happen to me... Again!). Having a "proper" table allows us to have a place to return to, have a drink, eat or whatever is necessary to change the mood before returning "to the ring."*

- Show/Live music

Integrating shows and live music is something that I believe is fundamental and enriches the experience, as well as being an integrator of the arts that make tango. Having musicians and singers revitalizes and feeds the entire tango ecosystem. I cannot imagine developing tango and inserting it back into society without integrating different arts as it did in its golden age, where cinema, poetry, painting, theater, sculpture, dance and, of course, music all interacted with society from different perspectives, generating a synergy in which one art lifted up the others and vice versa.

Cultural marketing

I want to share some observations that can contribute something to the promotion of tango to reach more people and to communicate effectively.

Currently, many of those who teach tango dancing publish and promote their services in tango magazines, tango websites, milongas and even in other classes (the latter is horrible but true). With this, the only thing they achieve is dividing the fixed number of participants, atomizing "the market" into smaller and smaller parts and reducing the profits of those who have lived on this for years.

> *The "cake" is divided into more pieces every time.*

With respect to the lessons, by not adding more value than the figures taught, the distinction made in order to compete with other *tango teachers* is a lower rate. This affects everything, since today anyone who knows how to make a few figures with a certain amount of prolixity can be considered a tango "teacher," competing with people who have been doing it for years and who are part of the history of the genre. I suppose this is happening because (except within the tango community) society does not have clear standards for evaluating the quality and representation of a tango teacher. I believe that this is one of the great challenges that exists for those of us who want to add value, make the community grow and develop the tango industry.

Others come to tango, learn something, get excited and soon they get a lounge, sound, print some fliers, make a *fan page* and they already have "their own milonga." It's worth saying that the people who call this new environment milonga are milongueros and apprentices who stop going to elsewhere to attend theirs. The problem lies (in my opinion) in that they do little or nothing to initiate new people and add people (consumers) to the tango community.

On the other hand, there's no business model behind the initiative, but only a few tangos downloaded from the Internet (in mp3 format), an invited DJ and a dance partner who wants to promote themselves for the "show."

> *That's the entire "business plan."*

I think we're not fully aware that if the milonga is organized into a club, for example, the people at the bar, the waiter, the cooks and those who clean the place, among others, also have to get an income. It has to be profitable; otherwise it won't last and in fact, milongas are opened and closed by (among other things) this lack of planning and professionalism. If the organizer of the milonga only cares about the sale of tickets, he's not seeing that the owner of the venue needs to raise money through the sale of drinks from the bar (to name just one example).

All this seems obvious, and as I write it I have the feeling that "it's stating the obvious." However, today I still see people who bring their own mineral water and food (to places where water is sold, or there is a cafeteria or restaurant) and secretly consume it, just to save themselves having to buy it in the place. Then they complain about the absence of air conditioning or things like that. It's worth clarifying here that they're not homeless or unemployed, but I'm talking about people who maybe took a couple of months off to learn to dance the tango in Buenos Aires, and some even crossed the ocean traveling *Business* class and have several pairs of tango shoes to match their wardrobe ... I think the contradiction is clear, is not it?

> *Why when we go to a disco do not we complain about paying 500% more for the price of a drink, and when we go milonguear, which is something that fills our soul, we complain and want to save the price of a coffee?*

Personally, I don't think it's the fault of the public, but of those of us who have the opportunity of noticing and recognizing in the new consumer the importance of turning the wheels of the whole industry.

> *Tango doesn't have to be expensive, it has to be valuable, and those who "do" it have the opportunity to promote it that way.*

As for our "industry", I think it's time to come up with a way to promote the benefits of tango professionally and to have clear objectives to attract - and sustain over time - new clients. For this I consider the following necessary:

- To recognize that we have a business. It's time to leave behind the over-used expression:

> *"It's too commercial."*

It seems like it's sinful to charge for the product or service that we offer to the community. If we have a trade or business it's important to develop it professionally and leave improvising for the milonga floor.

- A clear offer where beginners are welcome and not a burden for those who teach.

- Milongas and "friendly" practices with beginners, where they can develop their training and gradually integrate into the community.

- An integrated plan that takes into account gastronomy, price policy, comfort, aesthetics, schedules, shows and live music, integration with foreigners (bilingual menus for example), tango clothing stores and designers, tango shoes, ease of communication, *easy to buy*, clear information on multiple platforms, transportation, accessibility, ramps for the disabled, menus for celiacs, vegetarian alternatives, parking, various methods of payment, etc.

- Marketing actions to generate interest outside the "tango circuit," integrating or initiating people who aren't aware of the comparative benefits of the practice of tango with respect to other recreational/cultural activities.

- To draw figures and personalities who can shore up the tango movement by inviting their "followers" to know it and integrate.
- Develop activities for the public and private sectors: universities, clinics, hospitals, guilds, tourism agencies, embassies (I think diplomatic staff should know how to dance the tango).
- To have a greater presence in the "non-specific" press for tango, in order to reach an audience with an original idea.
- Also use alternative approaches to "entertainment" for tango. Whether it's *ice breakers* as activities to break the ice in meetings or social gatherings.
- Promote further research and support of the medical or scientific sector on the possible health benefits of dancing tango, whether in regards to neurosciences, Parkinson's, Alzheimer's, physical recovery (kinesiology), cardiology, psychology, among many other disciplines that can reach out to tango to find a platform for work, support and research for its development and contribution to health in general.
- Human resources: social interaction and the complexity of learning tango represents a great opportunity to obtain certain *insights* from the members of a team or applicants for certain

positions in a company. From the activity, specific facts or actions can be pointed out that are verifiable as indicators that the employer or team leader can later analyze. Taking into account the challenges involved in the learning process is an ideal platform to have as a reference of the behavior of the learner who faces new challenges, in circumstances and scenarios that are unfamiliar. In addition to checking his performance in the most immediate relationships (his partner/at a dance) and the environment (the other couples in the same situation). Here is a wide field of exploration that is waiting to be discovered.

Workshops for non tango dancing participants

The coach has the mission of creating learning spaces that represent a valuable experience for the participant, and for the person who engages one (the person who engages a *workshop* doesn't always participate in it, so it's good to distinguish it).

We must always remember that the client is our priority and that tango is a platform to facilitate the objectives that were planned before engaging the *workshop*.

To offer an activity that is valuable to the client, we must first:

- Observe.
- Inquire.
- Check that we understand what he's saying to us.
- Challenge his beliefs.

During the "warm-up" we have an opportunity to analyze the physical and coordination issues of each participant, so if, during the session, they succeed in successfully carrying out the different suggested figures, the *workshop* obstacles from that moment on will be directly related to:

- How they communicate with their partner.
- Beliefs about themselves or the activity.

It is a priority to listen to what the participant tells us, to discover opinions that (without being conscious) are taken for granted and not recognized for the fact that, no matter how fundamental, an opinion is still an opinion.

Use effective questions related to what the participant brings us as questioning, objections or annoyance both emotionally and intellectually. Listen to what he says and, above all, gently challenge what he "believes" (his opinion) and that which he is convinced of in relation to any obstacle.

Except for some figures that the coach suggests, most of the "warm-up" represents a personal and individual challenge. At the same time, it's essential to pay attention to the small details, which will provide us with information about the participants, from their state of mind, attitudes, eye contact, empathy, balance, presence (the here and now), interaction with other participants, level of excitement, repetitive patterns, facial expressions, coordination, body language and use of space.

> *Something wonderful that I really enjoy is when, at the end of the "warm-up," the coach giving the* workshop *suggests that couples form up to start practicing and "construct the tango embrace." At that moment (when the participants don't know each other), some start with furtive glances, embarrassed faces, and begin to "draw" with their feet on the floor, almost like children in a kindergarten. This is something wonderful and of incalculable value.*

At least on this day, they are in a situation where they're at the same level, where they're equal and none of their "credits" in the outside world have validity.

Whether they are millionaires, politicians, students or unemployed, they're in an equal situation that can be frightening or simply challenging and fun (in all cases, a good coach must be prepared).

The use of didactic objects such as necklaces with a luminous dot in the center of your chest, masks to cover the eyes, balloons and any other object that offers color, gives the day a playful and light-hearted component that allows the energy to flow between participants and, through funny mistakes or anecdotes, achieve empathy with each other and receive *feedback* from each other about the actions taken.

Also integrating mate, dulce de leche, some traditional Argentinian candy or "tortas fritas" can generate an emotional bond that will contribute to adding value whether we are working with Argentinians or foreigners.

I consider it of extraordinary value to coordinate all this within a framework of fun and learning, which turns the work of the coach into a work of art.

Depending on the objectives of the *workshop*, we will design the structure of the day prioritizing certain dynamics based on those objectives.

However, the common axis in all is going to happen to a greater or lesser extent through relationships and communication, key words and foundations that give a universal added value to our tango cultural plan.

Dynamics of nonverbal communication that include or do not include contact are a challenge to the mechanisms of the "perception" of the participants and the way in which they "interpret" what they perceive (which is not the same).

> *In this, any resemblance to the circumstances of daily life is purely coincidental.*

Playing with roles is also a very interesting point. Changing roles is a challenge that is sometimes underestimated, but I've witnessed (in addition to experiencing it personally) a change of perspective regarding my partner's position. The empathy and understanding that are generated after "putting yourself in the other person's shoes" can be revealing.

Look for dynamics that demonstrate that communication can be intangible, that is, that there is the possibility of dancing with a partner without any physical contact. It is an experience that is usually enjoyed a lot and also is very useful for them to reflect on. It is neither more nor less than discovering yourself dancing with someone in a rhythm that you didn't know until a few hours ago.

Playing with "embellishments" and the music represents a condiment for the senses and a stimulus for the different personalities of each person. The challenge here consists of the ability of the leader to offer a space to the *follower* to express (with physical movements) what he hears about the music. It is worth clarifying that the musical selection will play an important role to provide a range of possibilities in the interpretation of different voices, instruments and sounds.

The famous "exchange of dance partners" has a mystique, because when couples are beginning to take hold, a change is suggested. For some it means to start again, for others it means to simply adjust some details to get back to achieving a fluid communication. That the participants take advantage of this dynamic and don't struggle with it (at least without learning anything) is the responsibility of the coach as the leader of that dynamic.

140

Benefits associated with Tango dancing

- Individual: Anyone can go alone, both men and women, but you can also go as a couple or in a group. It is a favorable place to meet people from all over the world and with the most varied interests. The milongueros codes make interaction easier because of "the cabeceo" and the intervals between the tandas allow communication between the two dancers who have just met. Otherwise, anonymity is another accepted form, since the idea is to dance and, once the session is over, everyone returns to their place or is free to invite another person to dance.

- Social: Parents, children and grandparents can go. They can dance with each other or with others. There are no social or economic differences.

- Dancing in a milonga implies a code of coexistence and mutual respect that includes not only the relationship with the dance partner but also with the rest of the couples that are dancing around. Because of that, it's very important and valuable to respect the spaces and the "sense of circulation" (anti-clockwise) of the dancers on the dance floor

- Variety: There are milongas and practices for all tastes, with very different codes and styles. There are noon-late-afternoon and evening, there are live orchestras, with a dancers show, with a parquet floor, tiles and the most diverse surfaces. There are outdoors, there is places to go in "slippers" and "classy sporty," with cabeceo and without. There are *queer* or *gay friendly*. There are tangos from the thirties and modern tangos.

- Comprehensive: Tango involves not only dance, but also other scenic arts, linguistics (slang), literary, musical, cinematographic, costumes, sculptures, paintings, etc.

- Health: It has been proven that dancing the tango brings health benefits. Studies from professionals from all over the world affirm this.

In my opinion, there are few activities that combine so many benefits in an immediate, economic, accessible, universal and original form like tango. It is not in vain that it is danced and listened to, all over the world.

I understand that it is very important to find recreational spaces in society that promote the development of virtues that involve social, individual and physical aspects, allowing people to balance different aspects of their lives.

144

Epilogue

To conclude the first edition of this work, I think it's useful to emphasize the value of "the human." We live in times when "artificial intelligence" plays chess, drives cars, and is entering the fields of medicine and law, among many others.

On the other hand, I think that many of us stop "learning," at least voluntarily, when we receive a degree, be it university or at the level we've chosen for our career. Much of this learning is based on logical abilities, leaving aside other more primitive and ancestral (but no less important) *emotions, social* and *empathic abilities* (necessary to constitute ourselves as the social beings we are). I think many of us stopped dancing, doing magic, acting and challenging our creativity a long time ago...

Today, I think that a sense of humor, human warmth and emotional skills will begin to make a difference in society, becoming a very valuable asset.

Those of us who dance tango have great training in hugging human beings.
Let's share it!

146

Glossary

1) Tango: It is a musical genre and dance, characteristic of the Rio de la Plata region and its area of influence, mainly from the cities of Buenos Aires in Argentina and Montevideo in Uruguay.

2) Milongas: Places where tango or tango rhythm is played in 2/4 time.

3) Practices: Milongas with more lax codes where you can practice steps or dance different styles. Normally the clothing is casual and tangos are continued, without being separated by a "cortina."

4) Styles of tango: There are different ways of dancing the tango, with variations among them of the dancers' embrace and the steps that are used to follow the musical rhythm.

5) Tango steps: These are sequences of characteristic steps that are used to dance the tango.

6) Milonguear: Go dancing the tango at a social milonga.

7) Milongueros code: Guidelines or rules that are used within a milonga, such as the "cabeceo."

8) Periods in the history of the tango: The "Old Guard" (1895-1925) and the "New Guard" (1925-1950). The forties is considered the *golden age* of tango.

9) Tanda: This is the name given to the execution of four consecutive tangos of the same rhythmic style or orchestra. They are separated from each other by a non-danceable musical theme, which is usually not tango, called a "cortina." You are normally invited to dance a full tanda.

10) The embrace: This is a fundamental factor in order to dance. It is made between the members of a couple who are going to dance and may vary according to the separation of the torsos of both dancers and/or the style they want to interpret.

11) DJ: *Disc-jockey*.

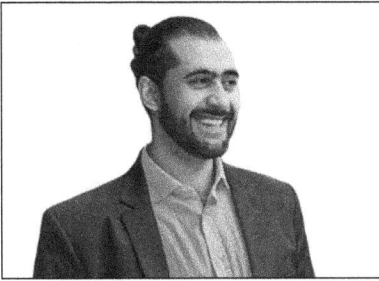

Adrián Luna is Certified Ontological Coach, speaker and social dancer. He has been involved with tango since his adolescence and, as a result of his experience, he is challenging the current learning model by proposing the *Coach* as an alternative to "tango steps teachers." He has given talks, workshops and tango workshops in Argentina and Europe, with primary school children, at universities and at cultural centers, among other places.

adrianlunacoach.com

Thank you!

www.ingramcontent.com/pod-product-compliance
Lightning Source LLC
Chambersburg PA
CBHW071857020426
42331CB00010B/2559